HEALING HEARTS

Healing Hearts

The Journey from Grief to Grace

Valerie Lynn

4-P Publishing

Valerie Lynn
Chattanooga, TN
valerieb22@outlook.com
@valynn12 via Twitter (Val Lynn)
www.healinghearts16.com

Published by 4-P Publishing

ISBN: 978-1-941749-68-5

Typesetting services by BOOKOW.COM

*I dedicate this book to my beautiful mother Mary Patrick Brown whose love is unconditional. I also dedicate this to women who have lost a child. I acknowledge you. I see you and you matter. A very special thank you goes out to, Tara McDaniel, Erica Whetstone, **Evangelist Luella Anthony Patrick, LaTorra & Carol Dean**, Terry Murden, Kendal Murden, Tabitha Wiggins, Wanda Boyd, Veronica Houston, Marilyn Boyd, Angela Nelson, Demetra Scruggs, Carlton Patrick and to the rest of my family and supportive friends.*

Contents

Introduction

I am an ordinary woman, who lives an ordinary life, into which something extraordinary happened. My story is one of wrong choices, painful loss, redemption, and a new spiritual awakening to live once again. I decided to share my story in hopes it will give other women a voice who have endured child loss and found or are still seeking healing in its journey.

After 8 years of allowing this story to settle in my heart, I decided it was time to share it with those who have also experienced this journey in hopes they too may find healing and support. Writing this book has allowed me to speak freely about my journey without the stigma of shame or guilt.

In these next chapters, I will take you on my journey of the brokenness I suffered, the loss of my belief system and the tragedy that became a miracle in the making. The following chapters are excerpts from my daily journal. Lend me your ear and your heart and follow me on the journey of healing hearts one moment at a time.

And Life Goes On

A UGUST 20, 2008, she came struggling into this world and passed peacefully out of this world. My child, Zora Lynn, lived only minutes that day. I was childless. I was not expecting to come home with empty arms and a loneliness that would consume my life. That very moment I realized I was childless, was the day I felt my life was over. I consciously made the decision to stop living. I remember sitting in my bedroom, with only the light from the window glaring inside my small apartment. I sat motionless staring at the blank screen on the television. I was here, but I was not. I remember looking at my Bible, which I keep near my bed, reaching for it and quickly pulling away. In that, instant I turned away from GOD. Who does that? Well, I did. How could He let this happen to me? How could He let this happen to His child? In my mind, if He turned away from me, I would turn away from Him. Therefore, in that moment, I turned away from God and decided to stop living.

In this haze of loss and confusion, I turned to food, and anything else self-destructive that would take me away from this planet.

Let's go back a little. Back to the day, before the doctors told me something was wrong with my unborn child. Back when, that part of me knew what was about to happen, but admittedly did not want to claim the truth. The day before I went into the hospital, I had a scheduled ultrasound with a new doctor in my town. I left work early that morning with an uneasy feeling in my entire body. I was overly exhausted, and my swollen feet made it hard to walk. Each step I made seemed painful. I went into the examination room, changed into those awful backless gowns and laid face up on the table. The nurses rubbed the gel on my belly as I looked at the enormous monitor overhead. The nurse said "hmm." With that, I knew it was a confirmation of what I did not want to claim. In my spirit, I knew something in my body wasn't right. I could feel the physical struggle inside. There was little movement in my belly surrounded by an inadequate amount of fluids. It was if my child was floating in the shallow end of the pool, gasping for air. That image! God, that image!

I remember my doctor telling me we need to get you to a specialist as soon as possible. I heard him talking, yet I did not. I lost some reality because my thoughts were focusing on returning to work before I had missed too much time. My doctor and I made the appointment with the specialist for the following morning.

As I walked to my car, my footsteps became lighter and lighter. I made it to my car, and the tears began to run down my face. For a moment, it was as if I was walking on air. I made it all the way to the building exit and almost stumbled. I took a seat on the nearest waiting bench and took a breath. "If only I could make it to my car" was my thought process. In all this, I was alone. The baby's father had abandoned me. I was alone, alone walking, alone worrying, alone trying not to give up! I made it to my car and sat there for what seemed like an eternity. I took another breath, started the car, and returned to work. As soon as I walked into my job, I headed straight to the break room. Sitting in a distant corner, I just stared at the wall. I remember images and people walking by, but a big part of me was absent. Every action I took after was as if I was on autopilot. The following day I was admitted to the hospital.

The next morning I went to the specialist's office with demolished hope. Soon after they examined me, I was placed in a wheelchair, taken upstairs to a hospital room and admitted (under duress). The doctors would not allow me to go home to gather an overnight bag or any of my personal effects. Of course, I cried and screamed at them to let me go, but they were in control at this point. I reeked of fear.

My fear of doctors and hospitals increased my blood pleasure over its limit. Admitted to the hospital, and diagnosed with pre-eclampsia, I feared for not only myself but also my child. Before I knew it, the doctors had both my arms covered with see-through tentacles containing IV solutions and both of my legs were trapped in some sort of device that stimulated the blood circulation in my legs. I felt as though I was strapped to the hospital bed and couldn't escape. There I was, surrounded by doctors, & nurses, and no God in sight. My mind was so overwhelmed that I could not hear Him. I could not feel Him. This journey I could not understand. I could only hear the doctor say there was a small chance we could save your baby so we must focus on saving your life. Why didn't I have a choice? Why was my life so much more important than my child's? Up to this point, I had lived an enjoyable life, with only a few bumps and bruises on the way. I would have given anything for her to see this world. Yes, even my life.

About four hours into my hospital stay, the doctors gave me medication to induce labor. There were so many people (nurses, doctors, & interns) around talking and poking and prodding, that I could not get a grip on reality. Not the reality I once knew. This was the first time I had no control over any aspect of my life. At this point, I believed, God was silent. I had been silenced! Later that night, I was administered an epidural, but it was not effective. I felt every pain, every back-breaking contraction! It was like, someone had a fist clutched around my spine and was not letting go. A few hours later, she arrived. Zora was here. The doctors quickly carried her away in what seemed to be bags and maybe blankets. The moments after this, are a little blurry. I cannot, or I will not allow myself to remember what exactly happened next. I do know a while later I gathered the courage to hold her in my arms and give her back to God. See there was some part of me that still wanted to believe! Even through the chaos, I wanted to believe that God, our God had not left me. Even though my closeness to God seemed to be deteriorating, my hope was that HE would guide Zora to his kingdom.

As with all bad news, we tend to lose complete focus of reality. And this reality sucked!!!! No other words can describe it. Little did I know the moment I turned away from God, He was working on me. He was working on restoring my life and working on restoring my soul and my bro- ken spirit. The problem was I was so deep in my depressed state I could barely breathe. It would take time for me to see the light at the end of this dark tunnel.

The Battle for My Life

A FTER the loss, the battle for my life began, and the choice was clear. Either fight or flight. Against doctor's orders, I checked myself out of the hospital and returned home in less than a week's time.Of course, there were other issues, which affected my health. When the body has such a traumatic experience, it takes a while to heal. In my delicate case, the healing had not yet begun. I am sure if my mother is reading this she would not expect anything less. Mother always said I was hardheaded, and I must admit at this point, I truly was. Getting away from this hospital, which reeked of death, was my ultimate goal. At this point, I felt my destiny was to sink into oblivion. Yes, oblivion. I wanted desperately to disappear. I returned home with only a few of Zora's mementos, but no Zora. No child and an empty soul, or so it would seem… but God.

I said before, I knew the people around me loved me, but mustering the courage to love myself again would be my biggest challenge. Loving me enough to fight for life and not give up was a test for which I felt I was not yet prepared. My child had died, and for many reasons, I felt it was my fault. My heart felt that losing my daughter was the price I had to pay for past sins of making the wrong decisions with partners and allowing my own selfish needs to come before what God wanted for me. I was one of those people that went left when God told them to go right. Living and breathing in a deafening pit of despair was my eternal punishment. For a while, the choice I made was flight. I tried to run away from this reality by taking sleeping pills and sleeping the days away. I even took sleeping pills during the day to numb myself to get through the work- day. However, my true comfort was food. Food was my primary form of escape. After all, I could control my intake of food, even though what was happening around me was far out of my control. With this choice, (yes choice), I wanted to accept my punishment and pay gravely for past sins (not realizing the price was already paid). At this point in my journey, I could not get a firm grip on life, as I once knew it and this sent me into a place where I called " The Land of the Nothing-ness." I will explain this Land of the Nothingness a little later. However, isn't it ironic how the ultimate promise for our lives can change us when disaster is all around? We sometimes feel so alone when disasters or devastation hits, not realizing through the pain and through the disasters, God is still with us.

The Land of the Nothingness

As I sit writing about my journey, the tears continue to flow. However, I must continue to receive closure. This part of my journey I dubbed "The Land of the Nothingness." The only way I can describe this Land of the Nothingness is that nothing felt right. The way I breathed, the way I walked, the way I talked, nothing felt right. There was nothing anyone could say that could help me return to the land of the living again. Part of my soul had died, and the feeling of loss was deeper than I could ever imagine. I have had other losses in my life, but losing my child erupted foreign emotions and reactions, and I was not sure where to turn. I fell into this Land of the Nothingness. The reality was, I still had to function enough to pay my bills, keep a roof over my head, etc. Therefore, I went to work each day to get the bills paid and rushed home to hide under the comfort of my warm covers. That rush home, to hide from the world was like a drug I had to have. The retreat from participating in life was my drug of choice, along with food. I consumed meals daily, yet I continued to be hungry. I showered, brushed my teeth, and covered my face with paint to keep up the appearance that I was ok. I had conversations with people daily, without being mentally present.

I went to work because it was something I had to do. During work breaks, I would stand in the stairwells and stare out at the nothingness. It was a quiet escape from the shuffling of annoying paperwork. Nothing I did before that made me smile or made me happy, felt good. Good things were happening all around me, but the Land of the Nothingness had its hold on my soul. My friend was pregnant and planning to give birth on my child's original birth date. Yes, we were pregnant at the same time (a miracle). This was such a wonderful time for her, but my pain was so great I could not show my support as a true friend should have. Thankfully, her child was born perfectly healthy. Part of my soul had died, and the feeling of loss was deeper than I could have ever imagined. I was no stranger to losses in my life, but none compared to losing someone who was part of my body. Honestly, I had to keep getting up in the morning for my mom. Having her find my lifeless body was something I was trying desperately not to let happen.

On the outside, I sported a smile, but on the

inside, the emptiness was getting deeper. I was damaged goods. The Land of the Nothingness had taken over. Nothing good is happening, and nothing bad is happening. You are just alive, walking, breathing, moving, alive, but not living. I could not feel life, as I once knew it. Every step I took was draining. A real test of my will came upon me one Monday driving home from work. At this point, I was still in autopilot mode. It was a clear fall day as I drove home from work. It is funny how things can be so clear on the outside, but jacked up on one's insides. There is a sharp curve in the road near the exit before arriving at my house. While taking this curve, a thought flashed in my mind. "Just let go of the wheel, ram your car into that light pole, no one would care." As soon as this thought manifested, I grabbed the wheel tighter with tears rolling down my cheeks and made it home as quickly as possible. I ran in the house and just curled up on the floor beside my bed and cried and cried and screamed and cried some more. My spirit seemed to be tainted, but my soul wanted to fight. I remember pulling myself off the floor and looking at the Bible I always kept near my bed. I could not open it, but the view of it told me something or someone else wanted me to fight. It was a battle between, why should I keep standing, and please keep standing. The battle was on for my life, and the first-prize winner would have the honor of taking home my soul. I knew there were people around me who loved me, who wanted me to keep smiling, keep living, and keep fighting. The question was, did I love me enough to keep smiling, keep living and to keep fighting, and most of all did I want to keep living. How could taking my own life be an option? It was clear that I was in a battle for my soul.

After my epic meltdown, I was determined to pick myself up. I had fought many battles in my life, but this type of deep and thick darkness was unfamiliar. I have always heard that the devil shows up the same but in many different forms. Well, if this was the devil's form, it was taking hold of my spirit, but I could not let him have my soul. Lord, I needed help. The gauntlet was down, and this meant war. Wow, but who would be the worthy winner of my soul…. but God.

Help!

There comes a time when relying on self only deepens the wound and drains one of all energy, negative & positive. Walking around on half empty was interfering with my job and my interaction with all those around me. One night while sitting on the floor going through my baby's keepsakes I stumbled across a pamphlet encouraging mothers who have lost a child to seek help. I sat for a moment looking at the pamphlet realizing there are no such things as coincidences. Apparently, the universe (God at His best) was trying to get my attention. I carried this pamphlet around for about a week, and at the end of the week, I made the call that would change my life and my way of thinking. I made an appointment with a counselor for emotional help. I remember this day vividly. Normally traffic was so heavy during rush hour, but on this evening it was smooth sailing. here were no obstacles in my path. I remember tuning into the radio and hearing a breaking bulletin, that Michael Jackson, one of the most dynamic entertainers of our time, had passed away. For a brief moment, I believed my child was in the company of another angel. I digress. I was somewhat excited that I made the first step by following through and arriving at the counseling center, but so many discouraging thoughts ran through my mind. "Will I be judged, will this person actually listen to me, will I be stereotyped for life, and most importantly, will I be known as weak?" All my life I have heard, just take it to God, and he will handle it, or therapists are for the weak-minded. Now, my response would be, 'didn't God create all mankind, including therapist?" (Self-discovery is a beautiful thing) I sat in my car for what seemed like forever trying to decide if I should go through with this. Who would be behind that door? Will these people really be open to my pain? Group therapy is something different for sure. Seeking help was something foreign to me. Usually, I was always the one giving the help, but receiving placed my heart and soul in a place of unfamiliarity. "Behold I stand at the door and knock…will you let me in?"

I decided I would seek this opportunity for help. I walked slowly around the large brick building and entered through the beautiful glass doors, stopping at the reception to ask for directions to the group therapy. As soon as I mentioned I was there for the session for parents who had lost children, I was given top priority and escorted to the therapy room.

As I said before, this therapy session was set up for anyone who had lost a child. I was expecting a few to arrive at this session. My counselor had mentioned a few more other than me would come to partake in this session. I walked into this room, visibly shaken and nervous to the core. Here I was, the counselor and I, sitting face to face. There were no distractions and barriers, just pure, unguarded emotional vulnerability. This part of the story is extremely hard to revisit. As I write this, I am taking short breaths, in order not to have a panic attack. I keep thinking closure is what this story will provide, sweet closure, God!

I digress. We sat for a moment waiting for the other members to arrive, but no one ever did. Instead of this being a group counseling session, it turned into a one-on-one experience that would help my soul to heal. I honestly cannot remember how the talking began, but once I started, I felt as if a big burden was about to be lifted. Here I was in a room worrying about someone (everyone) judging my situation, and it was not a factor. This counselor came to help me. Help me heal my broken spirit. I shared with her things I would never divulge to even my best friend. Also, she listened and cried with me. Someone cried for me and with me! This was such a powerful moment. She even shared her story of loss, so there was an immediate bond. The healing had begun.

Taking this first step to healing my heart was an incredibly powerful, yet vulnerable moment. It takes courage to allow a stranger access to your most intimate private pain. Alternatively, as most would say, your secret pain. I walked out of that session feeling as though an enormous weight had been lifted. For the first time in months, I could freely breathe again. For the first time, someone else wanted to help me carry my burden. This was a literal manifestation of we are our brother's (sister's) keepers. I allowed someone in, and the result was learning to breathe again, learning to release the past, and most importantly learning that vulnerability can be a good thing. This would be an ongoing process, and it was up to me to put the work in emotionally if I wanted my heart to heal. I am not sure if time heals all things, but I do believe in time, things get better. I was in the process of allowing my pain to help those around me instead of it crippling my every move. Perhaps, just perhaps, as someone once said, your purpose is in your pain.

The Awakening

Slowly I began the healing process. Slowly, I began to hear GOD again. Sometimes when you are in the battle for your life, GODS voice becomes silent. Only when you quiet your mind can you genuinely hear His promptings and promises. This was a beautiful feeling. I had begun to realize I was not alone in this battle for my life after all. God was walking right beside me all along, but my pain blocked all HIS revelations.

Day by day, I began this journey of a new self-discovery. I was desperate to find my true self again. The self that currently existed was tired, depressed, and alone. Have you ever heard of the saying "sick and tired of being sick and tired"? Well, that is exactly how I felt. I was tired of living yet not living. The burden I was carrying was too much for me to carry on my own. I continued to work on the healing process and believe me it was harder than I could ever imagine. However, I was determined to put the hard work into living again. I discovered the practice of living would begin to take me on a unique journey.

For many who have experienced a tragedy in life, the decision to keep on keeping on becomes a conscious decision. I made the decision to get back up and to get back up quickly. Easier said than done, I know. I pushed myself to get out of bed each morning until it felt normal again. My walk to happiness became my daily goal once again. By this time, I knew I could not do it on my own. Some people whom I confided in were tired of my sad story (even though we all have one). Others just said, "get over it already." That was definitely a blow to my heart. How could someone be so cold? Truth be told, not everyone is meant to share your burdens. However, I did find wonderful, beautiful sister friends to push me, motivate me, and most importantly, listen to me without judgment. These women, along with God, helped me live once again. My friend, believe me, living it isn't that easy!

We as women were not created to shoulder this journey of life alone. This rocky road is meant to be shared with true loved ones or true friends. If you have at least one good friend you have hit the jackpot, but I had and still have several. Having a great support system pulled me out of my hole. I did not need 100 friends to validate me or to hold my hand. I only needed an amazing praying mother and wonderfully amazing friends to help me in my walk back to life...

A friend asked me if I had received closure. Honestly, this was the first time in years that anyone has asked me this. This was the first time in years I said the answer aloud. No, I haven't completely received closure. Many women, go through this tragedy and in time, have a second child. This second child often makes the healing process smoother or fills the void. After all, you now have somewhere to put that love that was lost with your previous child. I did go through a period of trying to have another child, but reality surfaced. The reality is I will never be able to give birth, physically, to another child again. This was a hard truth to accept for years, but now I have made peace with this fact. Although, I have had time to absorb this fact, saying it aloud once again gives me chills. I remember the first time I was given this truth and my spirit broke. However, time mended my spirit back together. Not even my family knows this truth (but I guess they do now) so, you understand why closure is a relative term for me.

My true test of healing always comes on Zora's Birthday. The entire month of August continues to hold me captive with all sorts of emotions. I'm trying to allow the words to flow so you can understand, but my spirit seems to become a little tired when I revisit her "Birth-Day." Time has made it easier, but on some days (like today), I become overwhelmed with emotions. Deep in my soul, I know this too shall pass. However, I always seem to dread this day. August 20th, the day my child came into this world and the day she left it. I believe I said this before, time does not heal all wounds, but it does make living with your wounds easier. I often sit and ponder how Zora would be now. Would she be extremely active running around with her many cousins and play cousins? Would she have thick black hair like mines by now? Would she have an imaginary friend and have little cute tea parties (only inviting her stuffed animals)? Who would she have been? I am sure those thoughts will never go away. With these memories come pain and sorrow, but also with these memories come a sense of joy. I take comfort in knowing I have one magnificent angel watching over me. That is the joy I remind myself of this day. I am trusting God for the bigger plan.

Zora's Life...What if

WHAT if my child lived? I often imagine what my little Zora Lynn would be like. I can see her today, running around the yard playing with her little cousins and play cousins. I can see her getting into quiet trouble. You know, the trouble children often get into when they believe mom is not watching. Sneaking extra cookies, rummaging through mom's purse and opening anything that looks shiny and exciting, would probably be what she would be doing as a little curious child. I can imagine so many things if she were alive, but mostly tucking her in at night. Tucking her in when the busy day is over, and it's just us two. I would sing her a beautiful lullaby, and as she drifts off to sleep, I would look in awe at her beautiful brown face, cute chubby fingers and little toes, not to mention her thick black curly hair (which I know would have been so hard to manage as she grew). I was never good at styling little girl's hair, but I would've made due. I imagine she would have been the mirror image of me. She would have the same fiery, no-nonsense stubbornness, yet quiet grace. Yes, I can imagine what if now, knowing that in this reality she is still all those things, but just sleeping with a higher power. She's now my angel.

What I Know for Sure

EVERYONE has a unique, individual journey. Everyone has a path to take to become who or what the Creator deemed us to become. We all have different paths to take, and different roads to maneuver. It just so happened my journey was harder than I would have chosen, but in the end, this journey took me places I thought I would never venture. It journeyed me through roads of loneliness, which at times had me wanting to end my life. It took me down the debilitating road of depression, where just brushing my teeth took all the strength I could muster. I traveled the road of self-hate where I believed I was not worthy of love, or to be loved. As I said before, this journey was a much harder path that I would have chosen. Nevertheless, is that not part of life? Finding out how strong you are during the storms. Is that not part of life? Falling, just to get back up stronger than ever before. My faith in God is now stronger and unbreakable. What I know for sure is whatever the journey, know that in the end, the sun will shine again. What I know for sure is pain opens the door to healing and from healing restoration always follow. Yes, this is a sad truth, but the best thing to come from this, is, I am much stronger than I ever thought I would be in this life. ime does not heal all wounds, but it does make the wounds easier to handle. I have my, woe is me days, of course, but in the end, I keep getting up!

There is not a day, which goes by that I do not think about the loss of my little girl. Admittedly, some days are harder to get through than others. I hear the news that a family member is expecting or a good friend is about to have a new bundle of joy, and I respond with gracious love for them, but inside a part of me weeps. However, the good news is, with each piece of joy I give to others, it has been returned to me in abundance. This, my friend, is all a part of allowing oneself to heal. On those days when you do not feel like getting up (and believe me there will be those days), find joy in knowing God's grace is sufficient. God's grace has shined on you with the gift of the morning.

Therefore, my friend, I end on this note. Al-though your loved one did not make it to see this day, you, my beautiful friend, did! This new morn-ing is a gift to you from Him letting you know He has not forgotten you. Although you may be in mourning and pain, rest assured He has not for-gotten you. God says there is a season for mourn-ing and beyond that season. He will give you the crown of beauty for ashes, the oil of joy instead of mourning and the garment of praise instead of the spirit of despair (NIV Isaiah 61:3).

Continue to hold on and just remember GOD has you in the palm of HIS hands.

I would like to leave you with a few inspirational messages of empowerment.

Amazing Grace

WE all remember that sweet hymn Amazing Grace. That beautiful hymn gave many people the stamina to carry on through life's difficulties. Through our daily lives, we will need that something to help us throughout the day. We will need that something to help us get out of bed when things around us seem gray or when we feel we cannot survive one more day or even one more minute in this occasional turmoil we call life. However, I have two words for you that will help guide you through this time. Those words are Amazing Grace. Yes, grace will guide you through the journey you are on, whether it is a broken heart or even a broken dream, my friend Gods amazing grace will lift you up and push you beyond your fight. Remember our Lord never said you would not go through the fire, but he did say He would not allow the fire to burn you alive while you are going through it. Therefore, mindful of His promises and His sweet amazing grace. This grace will get you through that minute, that moment, that second when you feel like giving someone a piece of your mind (and we all do) or when you feel like giving up altogether. God's amazing grace will help you make it. Take it minute-by-minute, step by step.

Remember, you are amazing, beautiful, strong, and well able to survive anything this world throws your way?

Psalms 18:2(NIV) The LORD is my rock and my fortress and my deliverer, my God, my rock, in whom I take refuge, my shield, and the horn of my salvation, my stronghold.

Live!!!

This morning I awoke with the BLAHS!! You know that feeling of "can I keep going another day." That feeling of, "I just want to lie in bed all day and eat ice cream feeling." I looked over at my bedside table, and I grabbed my Bible. The first thing I turned to was Ezekiel 16:6(NIV). "I passed by you and saw you struggling in your own blood, I said to you in your blood…". LIVE! This is exactly what I needed to carry me through the day. This is what I want to pass along to you my friend. Whatever your situation, whatever your struggle, LIVE! Do not allow your past to control your future. Of course, those negative yesterday feelings and emotions will pop up from time to time, but you do not have to allow it to control your destiny. Despite your past, make the choice to LIVE. Despite what the haters say, LIVE! You are a beautiful creation meant to break the chains of bondage and to LIVE a life without pain controlling your existence. You, my friend, were created to LIVE! So, shake off those blahs and LIVE!

Questions to Ponder

1. What storms have you faced or are you facing at this moment?

2. If you're still in your storm, what steps are you taking to ease your way out?

3. What miracle can you see in your tragedy?

Parting Words

WHETHER you're an aunt a sister, Godmother or sister friend, you are always a mother. It truly takes a village. I realized, in the end, I will always be a mother to my beautiful, loved ones, born not of my flesh, yet carried in my heart.

Resource Listings

- Theravive (Therapy-Discovery-Results-Life) 400 E. Main St. Suite 140E, Chattanooga, TN 37408 423-551-9916

- www.theravive.com/therapy/grief-counseling-chattanooga

- Association for Death Education & Counseling www.adec.org

- National Hospice & Palliative Care Organization www.nhpco.org

- AARP Foundation Grief & Loss Programs www.aarp.org/families/grief_loss.org

- The Compassionate Friends, INC www.compassionatefriends.org

- The Compassionate Friends of Canada www.tcfcanada.net

Valerie Lynn is from a small beautiful area in Collierville, Tennessee, which is just a few miles from the great city of Memphis Tennessee. She enjoys writing poetry, spiritual creativity, and creating positive platforms for others to be their true self. She has a profound belief, we were all created as equals to come together as one to shoulder each other burdens.

Valerie Lynn attended the University of Chattanooga at Tennessee and later completed her Bachelor of Science degree in Criminal Justice from the University of Phoenix. She received her Ordination Certificate through American Marriage Ministries in 2013 and received a Managing Conflict Certificate in 2010.

Follow Valerie Lynn on her blog: Healing Hearts @ www.healinghearts16.com

www.ingramcontent.com/pod-product-compliance
Lightning Source LLC
Chambersburg PA
CBHW060626030426
42337CB00018B/3223